IMAGES
of England

AROUND IVER

Iver Village on 27 May 1930. This picture was presented to the Parish of Iver Church Institute by Captain Norman Macmillan, who piloted the aeroplane from which the photograph was taken. Captain Macmillan was chief test pilot for the Fairey Aviation Company (whose airfield later became Heathrow). He had some thirteen years' flying experience, was an author of several aviation books and was also kind enough to give the then Vicar of Iver a thrilling flight over his parish in a Fairey III F aeroplane.

IMAGES
of England

AROUND IVER

Stella Rowlands

TEMPUS

Slough Road, Potter's Cross to Gallow's Hill, looking towards Iver Heath on 11 May 1928.

This book is dedicated to the people of Iver – past, present and future.
The Thames Valley Hospice will receive all the author's royalties from this book.

First published 2003

Tempus Publishing Limited
The Mill, Brimscombe Port,
Stroud, Gloucestershire, GL5 2QG

British Library Cataloguing in Publication Data.
A catalogue record for this book is available from the British Library.

ISBN 0 7524 2862 4

Typesetting and origination by Tempus Publishing Limited
Printed in great britain by Midway Colour Print, Wiltshire

Contents

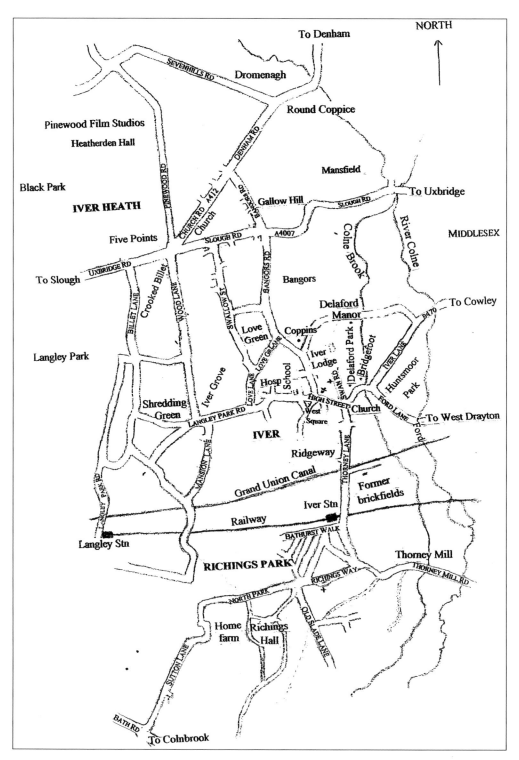

A sketch map of Iver in the middle of the last century, which relates to most of the photographs in this book.

Introduction

Iver is a South Buckinghamshire Parish, close to the borders of Middlesex and Berkshire. It comprises Iver Village, with Iver Heath to the north and Thorney (now Richings Park) to the south, but at one time the Parish of Iver also included Colnbrook and part of Gerrards Cross

Iver is an ancient settlement and evidence of Stone Age, Bronze Age, Iron Age, Celtic, Roman and Saxon occupation has been found. Some of this has been revealed transitorily by modern industry, but evidence of Roman buildings can still be seen today in the Roman bricks in the flint walls of the Parish Church, which has some Saxon features as well as architecture of later periods. That Iver's history has not always been peaceful was indicated by the Viking and Saxon spear-heads found in a gravel pit, and two ninth-century chronicles which tell of Danes fleeing from King Alfred's armies up the River Colne and being besieged on an island, identified by some as Thorney Island near the village of Eure or Ever. (It is not until 1382 that the spelling of Iver with an 'I' occurs.)

After 1066 the Manor of Iver, then called Evreham, was held by a Norman Lord of the Manor. The Domesday Book records land for thirty ploughs, three mills, four fisheries and two vineyards, with perhaps about 220 people. For most of its history the Manor and the Parish of Iver were probably the same (at least until 1862, when Iver Heath became a separate Ecclesiastical Parish) and major influences on the life of Iver would have been the Lord of the Manor and the Church. The community depended on agriculture and would have been profoundly affected by poor harvests or the Black Death, which probably did visit Iver between 1348-60s. Another major change was Edward III's handing over of the Church and the Manor of Iver in 1351/52 to the College of St George, Windsor, linked to his new Order of the Garter. Henry VIII made St George's surrender Iver to him and Edward VI granted the Manor and Rectory to Sir William Paget in 1547. The Paget family held the Manor for the next 200 years. Being convenient for London, many wealthy merchants, lawyers and those in Government service bought country estates in Iver, with its fine houses and farms. Sadly, several of Iver's historic houses have now been demolished, including Round Coppice, Huntsmoor and Richings.

Some industries have been notable. Brickmaking appeared at the end of the seventeenth century and was of great importance until the early twentieth century. Film-making at Pinewood Studios began in 1936 and famous personalities have visited or lived in Iver. C.R. Fairey of Fairey Aviation (which was taken over to become Heathrow) lived in Iver. During the Second World War the Hawker factory in Sutton Lane produced over 7,000 Hurricanes; aircraft vital for the defence of Britain. After the war, many industries developed on the Ridgeway site and the Britannic Cable factory became a landmark for miles around. Earlier, in the nineteenth century, Admiral Lord Gambier's gardener, Thompson developed the modern pansy at Iver Grove and A.F. Dutton's nurseries were famous for their flowers in the last century. Iver was then surrounded by productive fruit orchards. For much of the past, most Iver residents worked locally on the land, or in the large houses or shops, and much of their food was produced locally. Now most people travel elsewhere to work.

Being close to London and Windsor, Iver has attracted many famous visitors and residents. Queen Victoria visited friends and enquired about staff who lived in Iver. King Edward VII and Queen Alexandra stayed with Lord Howe at Woodlands. Their daughter, Princess Victoria, bought Coppins in 1925 and lived there until her death in 1935. Coppins passed to her nephew, the Duke of Kent, and after his death in 1942, his wife, Princess Marina, continued to live there with their family, Prince Edward (Duke of Kent), Princess Alexandra and Prince Michael. Following their marriage in 1961, the present Duke and Duchess of Kent lived at Coppins with their three children until 1972, when the estate was sold. Prior to this members of the Royal family regularly visited the Kent's at Coppins. Iver's Royal residents supported local events, and their anniversaries, births and marriages, as well as national events, were invariably celebrated in Iver by the ringing of the Church bells.

Other well-known visitors have included Samuel Pepys, who recorded visits to his friends the Bowyers of Huntsmoor in his famous Diary in 1660. Between 1710 and 1730, many famous writers and poets, including Addison, Pope, Congreve and Swift, visited Lord and Lady Bathurst at Richings. This tradition was continued in the last century by Martin Secker, whose firm published the works of D.H. Lawrence. He entertained many famous authors, including H.G. Wells and Sir Compton Mackenzie, at Bridgefoot. Earlier, in the 1820s, William Wilberforce, the pioneer for the emancipation of slaves, used to visit his friends the Revd Edward Ward and Admiral Gambier. At the beginning of the last century, Cecil Rhodes, the founder of Rhodesia, visited his sister, Miss Rhodes, at Iver Lodge and, nearby at Grove House, lived engineer and author Col. John Henry Patterson.

The pictures in this book cover mainly the past 150 years. The scope has been influenced by my own collection and the pictures people have offered in response to appeals. Sadly some country houses, farms and churches are not represented. If your particular interest has not been covered, and you have further pictures or information, please pass them on. However, hopefully here, long-term residents of Iver will enjoy recognising old friends and places, and new residents will see something of the contribution of predecessors and understand some of the derivations of names of local places. Much of Iver has been shaped by those who have gone before. Today Iver has been drastically changed and is continually under threat from demands from outside. Development, increasingly heavy traffic and industrial, motorway and airport expansion all have major consequences for life in Iver. It is hoped that some of our unique heritage can be preserved for those who come after us.

Stella Rowlands

Roman bricks in the junction of the nave and chancel of St Peter's Church, being pointed out by the Vicar, the Revd Francis Cobb, in 1930. Because it is difficult to make angles in flint, it is thought that the early builders used bricks from nearby disused Roman buildings. the tomb within the railings is that of Thomas Colborne of Iver Grove and it is the only Grade II listed memorial in the churchyard.

One

Countryside
and Work

Approach to Iver from Uxbridge and West Drayton.

Iver was once surrounded by fields and orchards and most people worked locally. This is a 1950s view of Iver Church, from the north-east approach to the village from Uxbridge (B470) and from West Drayton via Iver Ford. Before the 1960s, the tree-lined Iver Lane was joined by Ford Lane (left) and the road passed over the old Colne Brook bridge at Bridgefoot. Iver Lane was later rerouted over a modern bridge to cope with heavy traffic, and then the road was further modified by the building of the M25.

The bridge over the Colne Brook at Bridgefoot, taken from the church tower, looking north, in the 1960s. The bridge is shown surrounded by trees, some of which have now succumbed to Dutch elm disease or been lost through reconstruction of roads. The poplars at the centre back are thought to have been planted by the architect G.F. Bodley during his residence at Bridgefoot from 1899 to 1907.

Bridgefoot House and Iver Bridge photographed by the Revd Francis Cobb on a summer's day in the 1920s. From the bridge, the road continued left, up the Church Hill to the Village. This was said to be Queen Mary's favourite route to Coppins, the home of King George V's sister Princess Victoria, and later that of their son George, Duke of Kent. Queen Mary enjoyed watching the cows standing in the waters of the Colne Brook.

Milking time at Huntsmoor Farm in May 1975. Cows passed from the field shown on page 9, down Ford Lane to the farm for milking. In the 1950s, when the cows sometimes walked from a further field in Iver Lane, they would hold up the traffic at two o'clock.

Iver Ford at the end of Ford Lane, c. 1913. The River Colne is the County boundary between Middlesex and Buckinghamshire. It was fordable here for carts and horses and also had a footbridge, so was a useful quick route to Cowley Peachey, Yiewsley and West Drayton.

A distant view of Iver Church across the fields of Huntsmoor Farm in the 1970s. The construction of the M25, and the required rerouting of Iver Lane over it, means this view has now been lost.

Joan Kellner, of Grange Farm in the High Street and Blacksmith's Lane, feeding well-grown lambs in May 1931. Blacksmith's Lane led to a footpath between the fields to Richings Park.

Sparrow's Farmhouse at Love Green in the late ninteenth or early twentieth century. This 300-year-old listed building was demolished in 1994/95. The Sparrows, who had lived there for 100 years, sold the farm in 1984.

The junction of Love Lane and Love Green Lane in 1950s or '60s. While ponies Nigger and Wizard graze, the cows walk past for milking at Love Green Farm.

Cows in Love Lane going for milking, being herded by Sid Sparrow on his bicycle in 1932. In 1931 Sparrow's farm supplied the children of Iver Council School daily with a third of a pint of fresh milk in the morning break. The cost to parents was 1d per day.

Arthur and George Sparrow delivered milk from the churn to households twice a day in the 1920s. Some ladies used to have bread ready each day to feed the ponies when they called with the milk.

Haymaking at Love Green Farm, in the early 1900s. Hay left drying in the fields was once a common sight in Iver, and the scent of newly-mown hay around the village was marvellous.

Haymaking at Love Green Farm early last century. The dried hay was loaded on to a cart for storage for winter feed, often as haystacks around Iver farms.

Richings Park fields in the 1920s, with Mr J.S. Anthony's local herd from Home Farm, which supplied milk for the newly-built houses on the Richings Park estate.

The front entrance to Home Farm, Richings Park, *c.* 1929.

On the left—The cooling room in Richings Park Dairy

Right—Richings Park Dairy on the corner of the estate near the station

Left—Sterilising the milk bottles in the Dairy

The same scrupulous cleanliness is observed during the milking of the herd

A page from a 1920s book advertising the new Richings Park Estate houses, with the advantage of a local fresh, clean milk supply from the dairy in Wellesley Avenue. Mr J.S. Anthony's pedigree Friesian herd was grade A and certified TT (Tuberculin Tested). Milk was delivered to all parts of the estate twice daily.

A waterfall called Tumbling Bay at Huntsmoor, c. 1880. The River Colne not only provided fish for Iver's residents since the earliest days, but it was also harnessed by the Tower family to provide electricity for the house and estate in the early 1900s under the care of the engineer, Mr Clutterbuck. Before Pinewood Studios were built in 1936, Huntsmoor was considered for the film studio site and a concrete road was made.

The River Colne at Huntsmoor, c. 1880. There had been a house on this site from the time of the Domesday survey of 1086 until 1938 when the last mansion house was demolished. The Domesday Book also mentioned Iver's four fisheries, which yielded then 1,500 fish and eels per year. The River Colne is still popular with fishermen today.

On the Middlesex bank of the River Colne (but still part of the Tower family's Iver estates) stood Huntsmoor Mill, shown here in a painting by Lady Sophia Tower, c. 1840. A mill here was mentioned in the Domesday Book but the building above was the last working (flour) mill. It burnt down in 1873, in spite of all the efforts of the Uxbridge Volunteer Fire Brigade. this is the only known picture of the working mill.

Thorney Mill in 1939. A mill at Thorney is another of the three Iver mills recorded in the Domesday Book. (The third was also on the Colne Brook, just north of Bridgefoot.) In the eighteenth and nineteenth centuries it became a paper mill, in the 1920s a tube mill and after the Second World War it became a storage and packaging depot for a car polish company.

A rabbit shoot near Coppins in the 1940s. On the left with the gun is Vivian Edwards; George Stanley is in the middle. Several Iver men kept their own ferrets and went 'ferreting' for rabbits regularly. This, as well as controlling the number of rabbits, provided useful food for their families.

Henry Ewer aged 84 Iver Lodge August 13.1864

A rare, faded photograph showing agricultural estate workers, some wearing smocks, at Iver Lodge, owned by Martin Boswell, in 1864. In 1851, Henry Ewer, his wife Ruth and sons John and Thomas (also both agricultural labourers) lived at Iver Road in Iver Heath. There were other Ewers living nearby in Uxbridge Road.

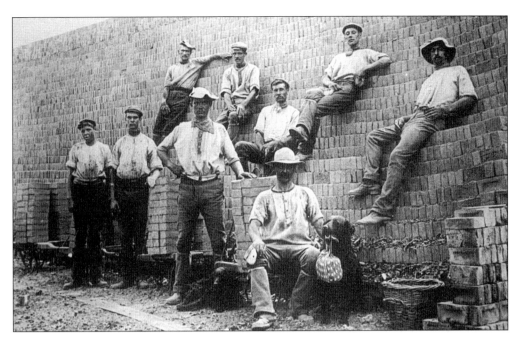

Brick-making as an Iver occupation goes back at least to the seventeenth century but it expanded in the nineteenth century. There was no shortage of labour and brickmakers were often poorly paid. Their children sometimes missed school to take lunch to brickfield workers, or to work there themselves. Girls as well as boys laboured, either helping make clay paste or moving and sanding bricks. It was hard, back-breaking work. In 1903 the pay for a fourteen-year-old girl was 9s a week for working twelve hours a day.

A moulder and his team, with one woman, in Iver brickfields. The moulder made the bricks (up to 800 per hour). He was fed the brick clay by the 'temporer' who prepared it, and the 'off bearer' removed the new bricks on a flat barrow to the 'hacks' which were long lines of bricks arranged so that air could pass through for drying.

Edward Reed and his son Edward Baron Reed ran a well-known Iver brickmaking firm from about 1870 to 1940. It was sited at Iver Court Farm and stretched as far as the railway and also on land where part of the Ridgeway Trading Estate now lies. E.B. Reed (above) is watching the bricks being 'skintled' for drying – each brick is placed diagonally across the one below. Wooden hack caps, shown in the foreground, were used to protect the bricks from rain.

Canal transport was important. Arriving at Iver by horse-drawn canal barges were raw materials for brickmaking: breeze (large cinders of coal and coke) came from Marylebone, chalk from Harefield, domestic refuse to fill in where clay had been extracted, and horse manure from London streets and stables for the fields. In return bricks were carried by barges to the Paddington basin. Here a modern narrow boat is moored on the north bank on the canal, towards Yiewsley, in 1980. The canal in Iver (Slough Arm) opened in 1882.

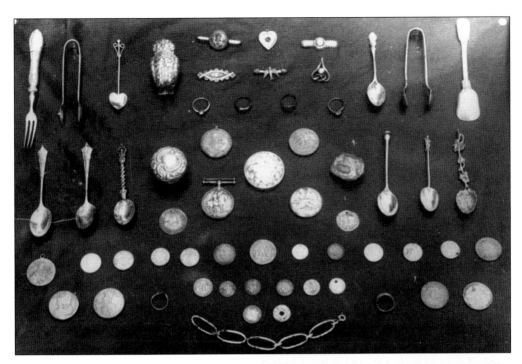

London refuse from dustbins was transported to Iver brickfields to be used as breeze for firing the bricks. This photograph taken at E.B. Reed's works in 1926 shows some of the items stopped by the screens. These include a Queen Elizabeth shilling dated 1571, one from James I's reign, a gold brooch valued at over £100, plus many spoons, rings, other brooches and a rowing club medal whose owner could not be traced.

Gravel extraction (and later in-filling with rubbish) has occurred on a grand scale in Iver. In 1928 these spear heads, held by a workman, were found in a local gravel pit being worked by Messrs Lavender & Co., only 2ft from the surface. They were identified by the British Museum as being of Anglo-Saxon (shorter, right) and Viking (longer, left) origin, which would have been attached to wooden shafts. They possibly represented both defenders' and attackers' weapons of over 1,000 years ago and are still preserved, mounted in a case in Iver archives.

Local workmen laying sewers at the junction of Love Lane and Swallow Street outside Love Green House, 1931. The name Swallow comes from the sink holes known as 'swallows' where drainage water disappeared.

Workmen at the Everlasting Tile Company on part of the Ridgeway site in the 1920s. The name of the modern industrial estate in Thorney Lane, Ridgeway, comes from a large common field which in medieval times was divided into strips, and on which part of Richings Park is now built.

The Dutton family of Dutton Nursery in about 1943. From the left: David, John, Mrs and Mr A.F. Dutton, Mrs Hedell, Peter, Mrs P. Dutton. They were famous for their prize-winning carnations and chrysanthemums, had stands at Covent Garden, and in the 1930s supplied flowers to the liner *Queen Mary*. The nursery fields, where at times many local people worked, stretched over large areas just off Bangors Road and also Thorney Lane.

Mr and Mrs Richard Talbot at Old Oak Nursery in the 1950s. After the war he pioneered the use of polythene film (instead of heavy, expensive, breakable glass) for lining greenhouses, making Dutch lights (tubular polythene covers) and also for pots for growing chrysanthemums and tomatoes. The $3\frac{1}{2}$-acre nursery was named after an old oak tree growing in the grounds.

When it was still a country lane – Slough Road, Iver Heath, from Potter's Cross to Gallow Hill on 11 May 1928. This photograph was taken before the road's reconstruction.

Pinewood Film Studios is a famous part of Iver Heath, though film credits often said 'Made at Pinewood Studios, London'! Heatherden Hall was sold in 1934 for about £35,000 to Charles Boot, and J. Arthur Rank and Lady Yule joined Boot as major shareholders in Pinewood Studios Ltd. Building of the studio began in December 1935 and continued, as shown above, into 1936. The company, Henry Boot Ltd, also built new houses on part of the Heatherden estate.

Pinewood Studios D Stage, 1955. The shooting unit for *A Town like Alice* on the final day. The film starred Virginia McKenna and Peter Finch and was produced by Joe Janni and directed by Jack Lee. Occasionally for some films, locations in Iver outside the studio were used and locals would be delighted when they spotted in cinema films very familiar areas transformed for the film story.

Innumerable local residents have worked at Pinewood. John Hargreaves, Financial Controller at Pinewood, is seen here walking across the superb 'Baker Street' set built for the 1969 film *The Private Life of Sherlock Holmes*. The set was cleverly designed in perspective so that the buildings got smaller to represent distance.

Pinewood Studios A stage in 1963 when the financial agreement for the film *Séance on a Wet Afternoon* was signed. From left to right: John Hargreaves (Financial Controller), the Producer Richard Attenborough (who also starred in the film), the Director Bryan Forbes (seated behind), the lawyer and the Production Manager, Jack Rix.

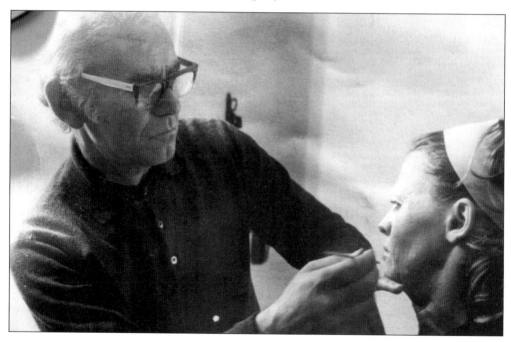

Bob Lawrence of Richings Park was a skilled make-up artist who worked at Pinewood and other film studios, and in his career of more than fifty-six years made up the famous. Here he is making up Julie Christie in the 1980s. One of his most dramatic achievements was to 'age' her from twenty years to over seventy for the film *The Go-Between*.

Two
Iver Village
High Street

Iver Village has changed almost beyond recognition in the last forty years, with new building, destruction of old buildings and more and more traffic and road expansion. This is Iver High Street a hundred years ago when, unlike today at this spot, it was possible for dogs and people to stand safely in the road. The Church and the Bull Inn on the right remain, but the cottages on both sides have been demolished.

Iver High Street from the church tower, at the junction with Thorney Lane, Iver Lane and Swan Road, *c.* 1890. In 1913 the need for a good signpost at the crossroads at Iver Church was discussed by the Parish Council because travellers unfamiliar with Iver would turn down 'Swan Lane' by mistake and the nearby residents were often being disturbed with enquiries for directions.

At the entrance to the village stand two public houses – a reminder of 1690 when Iver had fifteen listed alehouses, a much higher number than neighbouring villages. The Swan on the right dates from the sixteenth century. It had good stabling and carriages and horses of gentry were accommodated there while their owners were at church. In 1910 (above) there was also a cyclists' entrance.

The shops opposite the church on the corner of Thorney Lane were built in around 1771. One of these, just behind the signpost in this 1920s picture, was Polly Taylor's shop where the children of Iver purchased sweets and delicious ice cream. Her shop and the houses next to it on the right were later rebuilt. An Iver Village sign, painted on both sides by a local artist, was erected on this corner in 1951 to commemorate the Festival of Britain (see p. 115).

A rare picture of The Bull as it was in the late nineteenth century, before it was rebuilt, possibly after a fire. It was then owned by the Tower family but was sold in 1910 to the Victoria Brewery, Windsor. About this time the Bull was the home of 'Shaker Butler' who was famous for driving a four in hand horse-drawn brake. He provided a 'bus' service to Uxbridge. Hard-up villagers would sometimes walk to Uxbridge and then pay to take the brake back with their laden shopping baskets.

Iver High Street in the 1920s, looking west. On the right, with a delivery boy's cycle outside, was Boughton's butcher shop, which used large blocks of ice for refrigeration. Next was Rayner's chemist shop (later Clifford Wade's, which had large coloured-glass bottles in the top of the windows). Next came a shoe repair shop and, further down with ornate tops above the awnings, was once Choules' Store (drapery, clothing, boots, groceries, provisions). The next shop along with the awning in the distance was Axten's bakery.

On the opposite side, further along from the Bull and next to the old Village Hall, stood the premises of Walter T. Plested, carriage, van and cart builder, seen here in the 1920s. Wheels were made with iron, steel or rubber tyres. Later motor cars were 'painted and re-trimmed' with 'oiling done by contract'.

Iver Village Hall in the 1960s, shortly before its demolition when the outside railings had gone. Before the Village Hall was built, the 'Old Schools' (later the Church Institute and now St Peter's Centre) were used for parish events.

The High Street looking east towards the church in the 1920s. The Village Hall railings are on the right, with, in the dark foreground, the garden of the Miss Pearces, which ran alongside the High Street and is remembered for its large Monkey Puzzle tree. Choules' Store (with the ornate tops and awnings) is in the centre, with Iver bakery (nearer left) and, just out of sight in the left foreground, would have been Chaney's bakery.

HRH Princess Alexandra leaving the old Village Hall, followed by Mrs Lillian Weatherley after a Women's Institute bazaar in the late 1950s. The hall, opened in 1881, had a stage and was used for a large number of village events – concerts, fund-raising sales, meetings, parties, and wedding receptions. Those attending events were confronted by signs which said 'No alcoholic beverages to be consumed on these premises'.

Looking east towards the church in the early 1900s at buildings now demolished. On the right was the Miss Pearces' shop (white), with their garden (next to the telegraph post) and the railings of the Village Hall. In the foreground on the right was Weeden's butcher shop with cottages between it and Pearces' shop. On the opposite side was the village telephone exchange with the Bell sign and Chaney's bakery.

The two Miss Pearces talking to the Vicar, the Revd D.C. Welander, after Sunday morning service in the 1960s. On the far right the two figures looking towards them are Miss Florence James (Iver's own missionary who spent many years in India, and on her return worked in Thorney Lane police station) and Mrs Shelagh Thorp, the wife of the church organist.

Lester's fruiterers, greengrocers and hardware shop, which supplied a wide range of goods, was almost opposite the Village Hall in the 1920s and '30s.

Mr Weeden's butcher shop in Iver High Street in 1920s which, like Boughton's, provided home-killed meat and personal delivery to customers. Even in the 1950s Iver tradesmen were still delivering orders to customers. Bread, groceries and provisions were delivered regularly and the oilman with paraffin, Blackman's van with fresh fish and Burrows's farm lorry with fruit and vegetables went round local roads for housewives to go out and buy for their families.

Iver High Street in the 1920s looking west. Weeden's shop is just out of the picture on the left. Behind the wall is Mr Frederick Abbey's orchard. Both the wall and the orchard have now gone. The road and houses of Chequer's Orchard were built opposite the Chequers pub (about half way up on the right). At the top of the High Street is Platts Stores. The buildings on the right are seen more clearly below.

Iver Village Post Office was run by Mr W. James and later his son Edwin James. This was also a sweet shop and Dorothy Simpson (known as 'Dorothy dear' because she called everyone 'dear') served everyone with so much kindness. Some of the postcards in this book came originally from Mr James's shop. Next door was the Methodist Church, which had originally been Iver Grammar School. The church opened in 1888 and was rebuilt in 1963/64. Beyond that was the Chequers public house.

Iver High Street in the early 1900s at the junction of Bangors Road (right) and West Square (left). On the right is George Morton's grocer shop (later Platt's), with its covering of wisteria. On the left is the Garibaldi public house, licensed in 1862. It was once known as the General Garibaldi, and has now been demolished.

Next to the Chequers was Chadwell Brothers, a firm of builders, plumbers and undertakers, from 1840 to 1981. The front of the building was demolished in 2002 although the cottage behind, which is a listed building and was said by Chadwells to be one of the oldest in Iver, has been retained.

Morton's Cash Supply Store became Platt's Stores. Standing outside are Barbara, George, Josie, Mr Joe Gathergood (manager) and Mr Aylesbury, in the 1920s.

This picture of the Garibaldi (left) and Platt's Stores (right) in the 1960s also shows, beyond the Garibaldi, F.W. Jones (carpenters and undertakers) and Baker's garage (just in front of the conifer tree). All the left side of the High Street and West Square were demolished in the 1970s as part of the West Square development where new houses, the Village Hall, Library, School and King's Church are now to be found.

An aerial view of the top of the High Street in 1930. This shows how many orchards and gardens there were around the High Street then. Most of the shops shown earlier can be identified. The so called 'Broadway' is in the centre, with Abbey's Orchard on its left side.

The junction of Bangors Road with the High Street in 1925, looking east. On the right the gates in the wall lead to Abbey's Orchard and barn, which have now all gone. On the opposite side (just out of sight) would be the entrance to Iver House. In the mid-distance, past the post office, was a barber's shop and then Way's fruiterer's shop.

High Street, Iver.

The High Street, looking east towards Iver House and the Bangors Road junction (left), c. 1915. Fox & Son (grocers) was on the near left. On the far right was the Garibaldi, then the leather shop, Frederick W. Jones (previously Harry Jones) carpenters, painters and undertakers. Just off the right foreground in this picture would have been Baker's forge (later garage), Blacksmith's Lane and Grange Farm.

Mr Baker, the blacksmith, in Iver forge on the corner of the High Street and Blacksmith's Lane, in the 1920s. The forge later became a garage and sold petrol.

Shop and delivery staff of Fox & Son, family grocers and post office in the early 1900s. Miss Fox also ran a small private school. Further along, opposite Baker's, from 1958 to 1986 was Hazelgrove's grocer shop (see p. 60).

At the end of the High Street, opposite Widecroft Road, was Oxford House, another provisions shop. Here, in 1916, it was run by Elizabeth, the daughter of the proprietor Henry Charles Povey. She married Frank Timms who opened Timms' Garage in Slough Road, Iver Heath. Earlier, Oxford House was occupied by Charles Simpson (stationery, fancy goods, photography) and his wife, who was a milliner and a ladies' and children's outfitter. Oxford House is now a dental surgery.

Three
Churches

The ancient Parish Church of Iver, St Peter's, photographed by the light of the full moon by the Revd Francis Cobb in 1930. 'To effect this the camera lens was opened for forty minutes, the church having been focused on the screen of the camera before the light failed in the afternoon'. The other Iver churches are: St Leonard's (Richings Park), St Margaret's (Iver Heath), St Stephen's (Roman Catholic), King's Church (Free Church), St Andrew's (United Reformed), and the Iver Methodist Church.

A poster for the Harvest Festival in 1876, then held on a weekday in the evening. Harvest was an important festival and people brought a wide range of crops which they had all grown themselves. The fragrance in the church from all the home-grown produce was really marvellous. There was usually a large loaf made locally in the shape of a sheaf (see below, middle).

Iver Church decorated for the Harvest Festival in around 1909. The east end was usually decorated by Col. Meeking's gardener from Richings and the names of the ladies who decorated other areas were often given in the local paper. This picture also shows the gas chandeliers, electric light was installed in 1949. The text round the chancel arch was removed in 1913 and the choir pews removed in the 1990s.

Miss Faulkner's Bible class in 1910. From left to right, back row: -?-, -?-, S. James, S. Green, W. Jones, F. Cole, A. Foster, W. Hillier, -?-, ? Green, -?-. Middle row: E. Burrows, ? Grant, ? Clayton, Mr Simpson, Revd Gilliat, ? Gubby, ? Clayton, A. Simmonds, -?-, ? Garland. Front row: E. Wells, ? Green, ? Hibbert, T. Kedge, T. Smith, Miss Faulkner (housekeeper to Mr Gilliat), G. Stanley, J. Blythe, A. Sparrow, H. Munday, C. Smith.

A faded newspaper cutting showing hard work in the summer cutting the long grass in Iver churchyard by hand in 1932. This was a hot day and the refreshments offered by the ladies were said to be most welcome.

Three Vicars of Iver in 1926: Revd Francis William Cobb, 1924-1932 (left), Revd Walter Evelyn Gilliat, 1901-1921 (right), Revd Robert Noble Fergusson Phillips, 1921-1924 (front). Mr Cobb was an excellent photographer who regularly sent articles to local papers. Several of the pictures in this book were taken by him.

Choirboys with the organist and choirmaster, Mr Eric Thorp, 1932. From left to right, back row: Owen Jones, Bill Pope, John Cameron, George Johnson, S. Boughton, perhaps Ted Evans. Middle row: Ron Foster, John Chadwell, Eric Thorp, Ted Robins, Reg Foster, Front row: David Minchin, Reg Smith, Tom Hazelgrove, Dan Grant.

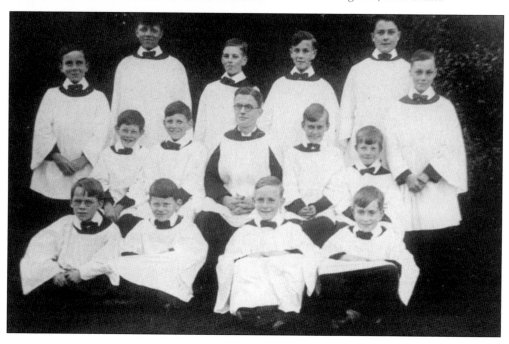

Drawing of the bells of St Peter's on their old wooden frame. In 1937 the bells were rehung on a new metal frame and the old timbers used to make the church lych gate, erected in 1938 in memory of Baron Anslow of Bangors, Iver Heath, by his daughters. The date 1621 carved in the bell frame timber can still be seen on the right-hand side of the lych gate.

The bells were recast and two new trebles added to make a ring of eight in 1929. Here all eight bells of Iver Church are seen on the church path. The earliest record of Iver bells is in 1552 when there were four great bells and a sanctus. The heaviest and oldest bell is the 17cwt tenor cast by Robert Catlin of Holborn in 1747.

The Bells of the Parish Church of St. Peter's, Iver.

Silent the great bells hang
High in the old belfry.
Help us to send their notes once more
Resounding joyfully.

THE RINGERS.

Sunday School classes in the Church Institute (now refurbished as St Peter's Centre), in the 1950s. They were winners of CEZMS (Church of England Zenana Missionary Society) shields for donations from weekly collections to a school for deaf and blind children in South India. Standing on the left are teachers Rose Munday and Dorothy Simpson, and on the far right is Juliet Binning. In the third seated row, Edie Stevens (Sunday school superintendent) is second from the left and Nancy Brench is at the far end.

Mothering Sunday at St Peter's Church, c. 1952. In the centre Peter and Susan Turvill give flowers to their mother, Mary Turvill. On the left Janice Blandford gives flowers to her mother.

Between 1986 and 1990 essential work was carried out to renew the floor in the nave and north and south aisles of St Peter's Church, by a team of volunteers led by Ted and Doreen Roberts. This shows the sleeper walls being rebuilt in the north nave in 1986 by Ian Martin, Roy Wattis and Richard Wattis. Many interesting vaults and tunnels were found under the floor before all the pews were replaced.

Looking west inside St Peter's, at a Sunday morning 'Children's Church' in the 1960s with a congregation of children, helpers and parents, and a children's choir. Since then, the early electric light fittings (installed in thanksgiving after the Second World War) have been replaced with modern fittings, the wall texts have been removed and the walls whitewashed in the 1970s. The choir and west end nave pews were removed in the 1990s.

Mrs Lewis Hall (formerly Meeking of Richings Hall) laying the foundation stone for the extension of Thorney Chapel on Monday 15 June 1931. The Revd Francis Cobb is on the left and Mrs Dennis is seated at the harmonium. From 1839/40 there was a building on this site which was used for worship and it was restored in 1874 as 'Thorney Chapel' by Mrs Charlotte Meeking, when a bell turret and small chancel were added.

Thorney Chapel was dedicated to St Leonard on 11 October 1942. This was the west end in 1950 before the new choir vestry was added in 1960. The name 'St Leonard' was chosen because there had been a chapel of St Leonard close to the old Richings Park House, although this had been lost well before the eighteenth century.

An early twentieth-century picture of St Margaret's Church, Iver Heath. Iver Heath became a separate ecclesiastical parish in 1862. St Margaret's was built in ten and a half months on 1 acre of land (which had been part of a field attached to Warren Farm) given in 1859 by Henry Sperling, Lord of the Manor. The church cost £2,645 3s 7½d to build and this was raised from voluntary contributions. St Margaret's was consecrated on 12 March 1862 by the Bishop of Oxford.

The church is built of brick faced with flint, in the Early Decorated style, with a tower on the south side containing a clock and two bells. The fittings were donated by parishioners, including the organ by Mr Edward Tompson (Dromenagh), and the choir stalls by Mrs Drury Lavin (Heatherden Hall).

West Square Gospel Hall (left) and Rose Cottage (right); have both now been demolished. The Brethren who used the Chapel held full-immersion baptisms and the water had to be supplied from the next door scullery; there was a cupboard there whose back could be removed for easier access. The new King's Church in the High Street has replaced this meeting hall.

Congregational Church Sunday School, Richings Park, c. 1930/31. It was run by Mr and Mrs Greet. From left to right, back row: Rene Cookson, -?-, -?-, Mrs Dolly Greet (behind), -?-, -?-, Peter Gardner,-?-,-?-, -?-, -?-, -?-, -?-, Mabel Maysmith, Shirley Fleet, Pat Gardner, Mr Greet. Front row: Joy Bird, -?-, Barbara Cookson, Diana Wise, -?-, -?-, Mary Greet , -?-, -?-, -?-, -?-, Molly Greet, -?-, -?-, -?-. In 1972 the Congregational Church (in Richings Park since 1928) became the United Reformed Church and in 1986 the name was changed to St Andrew's Church.

Four

Schools
and Hospital

Iver Village Council School, at the far end of the High Street, opened in 1897 for 200 boys, 200 girls and 135 infants. The 'New Schools' shown here in the early 1900s replaced various smaller schools. In 1828 Iver had at least eight small schools which taught a small number of children. In the mid-nineteenth century, in both the Village and Iver Heath, larger church schools were formed, which were further enlarged and replaced at the end of the century.

Anold water-colour painting showing the timbered school room over the vestry (far left) of Iver church in the early 1800s. A school was endowed by Robert Bowyer of Huntsmoor in the seventeenth century for the children of the poor to be taught to read and write. In 1821 this was enlarged to form a National School for sixty boys. In the early nineteenth century, the Revd Edward Ward, Vicar of Iver and a former naval chaplain, ran a school for the sons of naval officers.

The Girls' and Infants' school, next to the churchyard in Thorney Lane, was built in 1836/37 at a cost of £800 raised by parishioners as a memorial to Revd Edward Ward's ministry. This old drawing is the only one to show the school in 1840 before it was enlarged. New schools opened in 1897 and this building became the 'Old Schools', then the Church Institute, now St Peter's Centre.

The infants, dressed for a display around 1860, outside their school which, when built in 1837, was planned for about eighty infants. Miss Emma Goodey was the infants' mistress.

Girls of Iver School at the end of the nineteenth century. Miss Ada Wallis was the headmistress and the school was planned for eighty girls. In the 1890s children were sometimes absent from school as they were working in the brickfields. School records also show children suffering from lack of food and warm clothing. Through the generosity of Mrs Nicholay of Iver Grove, winter soup kitchens were set up between 1893 and 1895 at the Girls' School. Originally for the children, they were later opened to all for a small charge.

An Iver School class, around 1910, in the New Schools, built in 1897 by Fassnidge of Uxbridge. The Boys' School had earlier been in Thorney Lane near the police station and the Fox and Pheasant public house.

The 'babies' class of Iver School in the 1920s. The children are holding a variety of dolls and other toys.

Children of Mansion Lane, *c*. 1912. From left to right, back row: Ted Harris, -?-, ? Justice, Flo Bishop, -?- (holding flag), ? Justice, ? Bishop, ? Justice, Elsie Harmon. Second row: ? Justice with baby, -?-, Rose Wise, Dolly Finch, -?-, Madge Langley, -?-, Beat Bishop. Third row : Billy Harris, -?-, -?-, -?-, George Harmon (with bat), Nellie Langley (Fear), Emily Langley, -?-, Mag Brench, Doris Langley, Queenie Harmon. Front row: ? Castle, ? Castle, -?-, -?-, Maggie Bishop, Kit Blandford, -?-, -?-, Jim Blandford, Daisy Rolfe. (The Langleys lived at No. 6 Primrose Terrace.)

A very old family photograph showing some of the boys of Iver School. This was Canada House in the 1920s, with Canada prefects at either end. There were also Australia and New Zealand Houses.

Mrs Watling's class at Iver School, 1928-1930. From the left to right, back row: -?-, Ernie Burrows, -?-, -?-, -?-. Middle row unknown. Front row: Barbara Gathergood, Alfie Seagrove, -?-, -?-, ? Seagrove, -?-.

Iver School in the 1930s. From left to right: Lily Coppins, Les Povey, Vera Hazelgrove, Ken Watling, Doreen Hunter, -?-, -?-, Alice Coppins, Miss Stone, Henry Turblanche, -?-, Mr Stone (headmaster), Joan Denning, Barbara Burness, Dora Tuckwell , -?-, Eileen Parsons.

Empire Day 1928 at Iver School. From left to right: -?-, -?-, -?-, Mr George Stone (headmaster), HRH Princess Victoria, Lady Blanche Seymour, Mrs Cobb, Mrs Douglas (Mrs de Grey is out of the picture).

Gardening at Iver School in June 1932. The boys prepared and erected this greenhouse under the supervision of Mr Stone (fourth from the left).

Cup-winning team, Junior League 1946/47. From left to right, back row: Mr Woollett (headmaster) and Mr Neil. Middle row: J. Burrows, J. Cherrington, R. Seagrove, P. Povey, M. Stevens, A. Pearce. Front row: J. Snapes, N. Seagrove, J. Osborne, B. Pearce and R. Butler.

Iver School bell had remained silent for forty years before being restored, rededicated and rung again on 29 June 1977 to celebrate the Queen's Silver Jubilee, by ninety-year-old George Stanley (the Captain of St Peter's Church bells), joined by Ken Elkins and Tom Hazelgrove, former pupils of the school.

Kingsley House Preparatory School in Thorney Lane in the 1930s. The Principal was Mrs Butterfield and her daughters also taught at the school. The pupils wore grey and red school uniforms. This house was also known as Churchgate and was built in 1796. It had earlier famous residents including Jane Nash Linley Ward, the wife of the Vicar's brother. Her sister was married to the dramatist Richard Brinsley Sheridan, who had once expressed a wish to be buried at Iver but was eventually claimed by Westminster Abbey.

Richings Park School, Percy Lodge, in the 1930s. From left to right, back row: Peter Mabley, -?-, Hubert Nesling, Kenneth Elliott, ? Archbold, Bobby Lambert. Second row: Mr Kenneth Batchelor, Gerald Musgrove, Bert Preddle, -?-, John Cotsell, Donald King, -?-, Dick Seal, Mr William O. Betts. Third row: -?-, Kenny Boswell, -?-, Jack O'Connor, Gerald Eilouart, Peter Gardner, David Smythe, Patrick Cowan, Margaret Boswell, -?-, Peter Elliott, Bobby Musgrove. Front row: John Harrison, Derek Cowan, Rosemary Boswell, Charlie Bramble, Hugh Holman, Rex Darby, -?-.

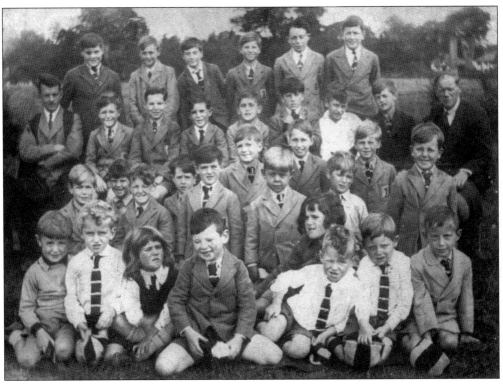

Iver Heath Board School in Slough Road in the early 1900s. Similar in appearance to Iver Village School, it was built in the 1890s and enlarged in 1906 for 214 children. Mr W.W. Ounsworth was its first headmaster. It replaced church schools which had already been expanded in 1872 to accommodate 100 children.

Iver Heath School entrance (on the right) in Slough Road in the early 1900s. The School was destroyed by a bomb in February 1944 (see page 78). The School re-opened on 1 March in the Village Hall, with some classes being held initially in Iver Church Institute and briefly Pinewood.

The Ward Memorial Home (left) and the first Iver Cottage Hospital (right) at the corner of the High Street and Langley Park Road in the 1920s. The Ward Memorial Home for the Aged Poor was built in 1898 as a memorial to the Revd W.S. Ward and his family. Seven persons could be accommodated, one couple and five single people. The tree outside the home was struck by lightning in 1975.

The First Iver, Langley and Denham Cottage Hospital, founded in 1863, was supported mainly by subscriptions and donations. The rent was paid and then the site donated by Lady Harvey of Langley Park. The poor of the three parishes were received into the hospital on payment of a weekly sum. During the war, in 1914, they also treated men of the King Edward's Horse based at Langley Park.

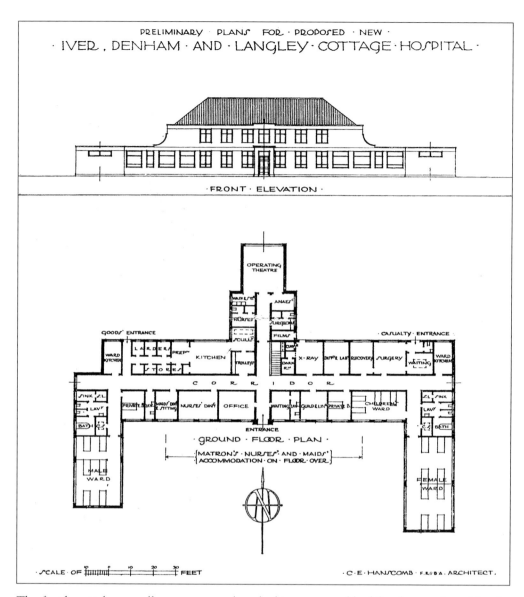

PRELIMINARY · PLANS · FOR · PROPOSED · NEW ·
· IVER , DENHAM · AND · LANGLEY · COTTAGE · HOSPITAL ·

· FRONT · ELEVATION ·

· GROUND · FLOOR · PLAN ·
[MATRON'S · NURSES' · AND · MAIDS'
ACCOMMODATION · ON · FLOOR · OVER]

· SCALE · OF ⊏⊏⊏⊏⊐ FEET

· C · E · HANSCOMB · F.R.I.B.A. ARCHITECT ·

The first hospital was really two cottages knocked into one and had first been enlarged by the completion of the Meeking Ward in 1893 and then again in memory of Col. J. Blyth in 1927. It had been officially re-opened in 1927 by Princess Victoria who became Lady Grand President. However the hospital was still too small (nine beds) and there was no room for expansion. A new larger hospital was needed. Above are the draft plans from a 1935 appeal. The new hospital was built from funds raised by public donations, on 3.2 acres of land at the end of Widecroft Road, given by Miss Georgina Ward.

The hospital was maintained by donations. Here the Rector of Iver Heath, the Revd George Harold Culshaw, is collecting for the hospital in 1928 during Ascot week. Other volunteers shouted to racegoers and day trippers to 'Throw out your mouldy coppers'. In 1928 £187 was collected in pennies alone!

The opening of the new Iver, Denham and Langley Cottage Hospital on Friday 2 July 1937 by HRH the Duke of Kent, Patron of the Hospital. He was accompanied by the Duchess, who wore a dress of navy and white. She was presented with a bouquet of red carnations by Gillian Saint, the daughter of Dr Stafford Saint, one of the hospital's medical officers. The Matron, Miss A.M. Darvill, served Iver Hospital for twenty years.

The Duchess of Kent often visited Iver Hospital, especially during the war years. Here nursing staff are saying goodbye to the Duchess at the main entrance after a visit in the 1940s.

In 1948 the hospital was handed over to the NHS. Iver residents fought very hard during the 1980s to save their cottage hospital, which was built by local donations and helped by local volunteers, but the hospital was closed after fifty-two years by East Berkshire Health Authority in 1988. It was later demolished and the site sold for development.

Five
Wartime

The Second World War Forces' Canteen at Iver Methodist Church in the High Street. Some of the troops here are probably men of the Welsh Pioneer Corps, stationed at Iver Grove, who were responsible for maintaining the smoke screens used to camouflage the vitally important Hawker Aircraft factory in Sutton Lane at Parlaunt Farm, Langley. From 1939 this was the main production centre for Hurricanes, building over 7,000 aircraft for the RAF. The last Hurricane of all to be made, called *The Last of the Many*, PZ865, was produced there in August 1944 and was used later for displays and films.

G v R I

HE whom this scroll commemorates was numbered among those who, at the call of King and Country, left all that was dear to them, endured hardness, faced danger, and finally passed out of the sight of men by the path of duty and self-sacrifice, giving up their own lives that others might live in freedom. Let those who come after see to it that his name be not forgotten.

Pte. Charles Edward Smith
Northumberland Fusiliers

In the First World War sixty-four men of Iver died for their country. Many others were invalided or died early as a consequence of active service.

BUCKINGHAM PALACE.

I join with my grateful people in sending you this memorial of a brave life given for others in the Great War.

George R.I.

The next of kin of those killed during the war received this letter and scroll from King George V.

Private Charles Smith, who is commemorated on the scroll opposite, was born in 1890 and lived in West Square. He was a rose grower by profession and played football for an Iver club. He married and enlisted in 1915 and was killed in action in 1917. His wife, Annie, also lost her two brothers, Arthur and Frank Furnell.

Fred and Jane Stanley and their young family in about 1916. He survived the fighting but had been gassed and died in 1924. (Iver historian and architect William Henry Ward also died in 1924, probably as a consequence of his war service for his country.) The younger boy here on his mother's lap, Freddie Stanley, died as a rifleman in the Second World War.

The Armistice Memorial Service on 6 November 1925, led by the Vicar, the Revd Francis Cobb. Iver War Memorial had been dedicated on Monday 14 June 1920. One of the most moving stories is that of the Green family of Oxford Cottages, whose six sons were already serving their country when, in 1917, the seventh and youngest son, Walter, on whom his invalid parents depended, was demanded by the Army too. Two of his brothers, William and Ernest, had already been killed and he was killed within three months of reaching France. After the Second World War another thirty-three Iver names, including that of HRH the Duke of Kent, would be added to the sixty-four First World War names there.

One of Iver's anti-invasion defence pill boxes, built in 1940, by the side of the canal.

Iver British Legion being inspected by HRH the Duchess of Kent in the 1940s. The Duchess worked hard during the war for the WRNS and visited hospitals, ARP and AFS depots, war factories and canteens.

Fund raising during the Second World War: the Mile of Pennies in Richings Park during Warship Week in 1940. Among those gathered are Mrs Standerwick, Mrs James, Mr and Mrs Page Turner, Mr and Mrs Ian Rankin, Audrey Naylor, Kathleen Robinson, Daphne Hewett, Paddy Turville, Marie Stengelhozen, Jill Beck, Robert Streeton, Pat Wilkinson, Pauline Weston.

'Spitfire Fund' Parade passing along Iver High Street, probably in 1943 during 'Wings for Victory Week'.

Iver's Volunteer Fire Brigade in 1938. George Sibley (fifth from left) combined his fire-fighting duties with work as a joiner at Pinewood Studios. Others included B. Keen, C. Bramble (a coal merchant who trained the crew), C. Smith, D. Miller and G. Alott. The first to hear of a fire would tell his mates who would pass the message on with the aim of getting six or seven men to a fire. They tackled fires using a coal lorry and a pump from Richings Park and then operated from Baker's Garage in Iver High Street. They were all volunteers and had to get permission to have time off work when there was a fire! The fire brigade was taken over by Slough in the late 1940s.

Servicemen having a meal inside the Plaza Tea Rooms, Bathurst Walk, Richings Park, during the winter of 1939/40. This picture was one of several found behind an old fire place in the Dana Bakery (once Plaza Tea Rooms) by Ole and Anna Hansen in the 1980s.

Iver bellringers in 1938. From left to right; Jim Blandford, Wilfred Munday, Bill Smith, George Stanley (Captain), Leslie Brench, John Barber, Fred Bettles, Bert Burton. Bell-ringing stopped for the duration of the Second World War throughout the country so that the bells could be used to give warning of invasion if necessary. One of the ringers, Wilfred Munday, a flying officer in the RAF, was killed.

One of the teams which manned the searchlights, pictured in Huntsmoor Park. Miss Butterfield from Kingsley House School, is the first on the left in the back row.

A unique picture of the Pinewood Home Guard platoon, a unit of the 10th Bucks Battalion, *c.* 1941. This and the photograph below were included in a publication commemorating the work of the Civil Defence, *Lloyds under Fire: a Tribute to the Civil Defence Services of Lloyd's 1938-1945*.

Another rare picture of a group of Pinewood firefighters and first aid helpers, *c.* 1941. On 15 February 1945 Pinewood Studios was almost hit by a V2 rocket. There was damage to windows and cuts to staff from flying glass but no-one was seriously hurt. During the war, Pinewood was home to part of the Royal Mint, the Crown Film Unit and similar units from the War Office and RAF. Pinewood was 'de-requisitioned' in April 1946 and returned to film making with *Green for Danger*.

A rare, rediscovered photograph showing the smoke-screen burners in Iver High Street outside the Garibaldi pub (now demolished). The smoke and fumes from these burners were most unpopular with residents! The Platt's delivery van is outside Platts Stores, opposite the pub.

Smoke-screen burners in the foreground in front of the van driven by Jack Barnes. The smoke screen was used for camouflage, especially for important sites nearby such as the Hawker Aircraft factory in Sutton Lane, which produced Hurricanes for Britain's defence. They also kept their own Hurricane fighter on site to protect the factory.

Iver High Street with the wartime black and white markings on kerbs which were needed during the blackout. Mrs Blake is standing at her doorway near the Swan.

Some members of the Iver Civil Defence. There were several Civil Defence units in Iver. In Richings Park the 'Local Defence Volunteers' as they were initially known, were affectionately referred to as 'Look, Duck and Vanish'. In October and November 1940 bombs fell in Richings Park, damaging houses and Thorney Chapel, and in Iver Lane a child was killed. Several incendiaries fell in the village causing damage to houses and shops.

Bomb damage to Iver Heath School after an air raid on the night of 22/23 February 1944. The bomb was dropped by an aircraft which had probably been hit by the gun on Chandler's Hill, and the school and school house were reduced to rubble. The headmaster Mr Bristow and his wife were rescued unhurt. By 1 March the school had re-opened in the village hall.

Windows were protected from blast by tape and blackout regulations (no lights to show) were strictly enforced. This picture shows the windows of Rose Cottage in West Square with Mrs Celia Lee holding one of her great-nephews in about 1942. Because it was not possible to 'black out' St Peter's Church properly, the times of winter early services in 1940 had to be arranged later in order to use daylight. Thorney Chapel, being smaller, had adequate blackout.

The Duchess of Kent, accompanied by the Vicar, the Revd Creighton, and the Churchwardens, Mr E.B. Reed and Miss Georgina Ward, entering the Parish Church. A memorial service was held on Sunday 30 August 1942 for the Duke of Kent, an Air Commodore in the RAF, who was killed on 25 August when his Sunderland flying boat crashed into a mountainside in the north of Scotland on a mission to Iceland. Their youngest child, Prince Michael, had been born at Coppins on 4 July 1942.

Iver's Book of Remembrance, which lists the names of all Iver's men who died during the two world wars. It was dedicated on Sunday 22 October 1967, in the presence of HRH Princess Marina, Duchess of Kent. Lessons were read by HRH the Duke of Kent and Maj-Gen. Grand, President of the Iver Branch of the British Legion.

A family photograph of an end of war party in 1945 at Kent Cottages. Among those present are, on the left: ? Hastings, Neville Seagrove, Ruth Moody, Gwen Moody, Ruth Sydney, John Field, Sybil Seagrove, Granny Kisslingbury (standing on left); on the right: ? Uzzle, Norman Seagrove, -?-, David Evans, ? Cowdrey, -?-, -?-, Faith Butler, Ann Butler, ? Simpson.

End of war party for Iver Lane Residents' Association, 1945. Most families from Iver Lane and Palmer's Moor Lane were represented. In earlier times celebrations were a bit rowdier. In 1815, to celebrate the victory at Waterloo, loyal Iver villagers put lighted candles in their windows and where such signs of rejoicing were missing, the windows were promptly broken.

Six
Roads and Transport

In the days of horse-drawn transport Iver High Street seemed very peaceful. A hundred years later this junction with Thorney Lane and Iver Lane is usually clogged with too much heavy traffic.

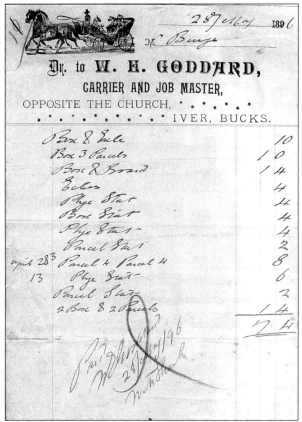

A water-colour painting of the junction of the High Street, Thorney Lane and Iver Lane, dated 1816. The churchyard has grazing animals, a gate in a different position and a signpost. In the middle of the quiet road boys play with hoops and a horse is unhitched from the cart.

A bill for goods carried for Iver School in 1896 by W.H. Goddard. In the nineteenth and early twentieth centuries carriers to Uxbridge and Windsor (and less frequently London) called regularly at the Swan, the Bull or the George, and were an important part of village life. Some Iver-based carriers were Mrs Sarah Marks and Mrs Sarah Simpson (1880s) and Alfred Lake and Ernest Simmonds (1911).

Iver had several blacksmiths'
forges – many took on cycle
maintenance and later became
garages. Cycling became popular,
but it must have been quite an
achievement to cycle down Iver
High Street in a long skirt!

A lorry leaving Weatherley's first
garage, the Bull Hotel Garage,
for the High Street in 1921.

Weatherley's Garage had several cars and drivers for hire in 1921. This is the yard at the back of the Bull, which formerly housed horses in stables.

Weatherley's Garage moved to the site in Langley Park Road in 1930. Hand-operated petrol pumps are in the left foreground.

Iver Service Garage in the High Street in the 1950s. Many years earlier this was a large Georgian house with a stable entrance, occupied, around 1910, by the Lake Brothers, who were motor and cycle makers and repairers. They also supplied oils, petrol and carbide 'at the lowest London prices'. A cycle could be bought on hire purchase for 1s 6d per week.

Iver garage (proprietor J.W. Thompson), which also had cars for hire, in 1930. Mr J.T. Buckland's funeral procession is passing the garage. In those days the coffin was carried by bearers down the High Street for residents to pay their respects. The cottages on the right link on to the Swan Inn, just out of the picture.

A 'Mogul' locomotive (2-6-0) pulling a stopping passenger train with clerestory stock carriages on the up line near Iver station in 1939. The engine cab window has been blanked off as an air-raid precaution.

The first passenger at the ticket office in Iver Station, 1 December 1924. Local rumour maintains that it is Mr Sykes, one of the brothers who bought and developed the Richings estate. The GWR Paddington–Maidenhead line opened in 1838, but Iver people had to use West Drayton station before 1924.

A Castle locomotive heads an evening express, possibly from Worcester, on the up line just past Iver station in the 1950s. Beyond the train can be seen the outline of the Plaza Cinema which was later demolished (compare with below).

Iver station in 1962. *Harrington Hall* (No. 5982, which entered service in 1938 and was withdrawn in September 1962) is on the freight line to the West Drayton yard. Despite the colour light signals on the main and relief lines, the goods line is still using semaphore signalling. On the site of the old Plaza Cinema the block of flats, Wellesley Court, is under construction. The Tudor-looking building is Alfred King, estate agents.

An Iver outing by Windsorian coach, departure from West Square (with drivers standing in the doorway of the Garibaldi). From the left: Mr Brench, Jerry Death, Charlie Crane, Bert Miller, May Crane, -?-, George Stevens, -?-, Connie Stevens, Bill Baker, -?-, Frank Pitt (with cap), -?-, Iris Hope, -?-, Derek Nevard, Tom Brench, Pop Davis, Mrs Jess Hope, -?-, -?-, Mrs Hope's mother, Tom Hope, Arthur Gosney (landlord of the Garibaldi, with trilby), Arthur Clark, Mr Woodbridge (with trilby), -?-, Mrs Bay, Mrs Evans, Mrs Chesterman , Mrs Lil Trevatt, -?-, Bob Chesterman, -?-, Sis Seagrove, -?-, -?-, Frank Grant, Alf Trevatt, Spud Murphy, Mrs Pearce, Mrs Gosney, Walley Dobson, -?-, -?-, Slen Seagrove, Mrs Vi Potter, -?-, Mrs Lou Dobson , -?-, -?-, Jack Potter, Bert Snapes.

Road-building over the last forty years has altered Iver dramatically. This is Ford Lane in the 1950s with its lovely view of Iver Church among the trees. This spot is now under the M25.

Thorney Lane (north) just outside the old Vicarage, looking south on 23 August 1937, before road works. The trees on the left were cut down to straighten and widen Thorney Lane. This view is in the opposite direction to the one below.

Thorney Lane (north) on 23 August 1937, before road reconstruction. The house with the balcony is Orchard Cottage (Colne House's gardener's cottage) and the building with the lorry outside is Colne Lodge, part of Yates' farm. Villagers used to go to the farm morning and afternoon, with their jugs for milk. All these buildings have now been demolished.

Another view of the widening of Thorney Lane, looking towards the village on 23 August 1937. On the left are cottages and the rebuilt Fox and Pheasant public house which re-opened in 1932. Between that and Yates Farm were the Barnes family orchards leading up to orchards and other land owned by Miss Ward. On the right the houses of Victoria Crescent and Marina Way are being built on allotments.

A narrow and peaceful Thorney Lane (south) by the railway bridge on 3 July 1936, prior to widening and straightening.

Five Points crossroads from Church Road (A412), Iver Heath on 1 December 1936. This shows the field opposite before the new Crooked Billett public house was built.

A picture taken from the same point in 1937 showing the new thatched Crooked Billet which had just been built. The modern large roundabout at Five Points was not constructed until the 1960s.

Five Points, Iver Heath, from the Uxbridge direction (A4007) looking towards Slough, on 1 December 1936. On the left, the Crooked Billet had not yet been built on the Wood Lane corner. The sign there points to the new Pinewood Film Studios. The house on the opposite corner in Fulmer Road, renamed Pinewood Road, is 'Point-in-View' which was soon demolished for road widening, and, eventually, the modern roundabout and the dual carriageway to Slough were made.

Five Points from Slough looking towards Uxbridge in 1936/37. On the left are Fulmer Road (Pinewood Road) and Church Road with the characteristic trees on the corner. On the right is Wood Lane. Other pictures of the Slough Road (A4007) before reconstruction, are on pages 4, 26 and 128.

Seven

Houses Great
and Small

Bridgefoot House, *c*. 1900. It was owned by the Tower family from 1700 to 1922, and from then until the present by the Secker family. There were many famous tenants at Bridgefoot, including, about the time of this picture, the architect G.F. Bodley. In the days of Martin Secker, the publisher, many well-known authors visited him at Bridgefoot.

A painting of the Elizabethan Delaford Manor. The house on this site, beside the Colne Brook, had been the home of the Ford, Blount, Lawrence, Tash and Young families until purchased by Charles Clowes. He demolished the house here at the end of the eighteenth century. Only the dovecote (now Grade II listed) which once had tiers for 500 birds, remains of this original building.

The new Delaford Manor. Christopher Tower bought Delaford from Charles Clowes in 1869 and built this new house, shown here around 1875. On the right is the Colne Brook which flows down to the site of Iver Mill and Bridgefoot House.

Delaford Park House (opposite the church) in the mid-nineteenth century, a painting from Lady Sophia Tower's album. Before Charles Clowes Sr bought the house around 1788 and renamed it Delaford, it was called Iver House or Hill House, and this is possibly the site of the Manor House of Iver, owned by the Pagets. Delaford Park House was burned down on 18 September 1856 and the whole estate sold to Christopher Tower in 1869 on the death of Charles Clowes Jr.

Christopher Tower built a new Delaford Park House, shown above, around 1875. This house was pulled down around the middle of the last century and the television and film star Sid James built a modern house (also now recently rebuilt) on the site and lived there for many years.

Huntsmoor House, *c*. 1880. There had been a house on this site since Domesday times. In 1660 Samuel Pepys records in his famous Diary visits to his friends the Bowyers. Even in the 1920s the house still had a Samuel Pepys suite where he was said to have written his diary entries. Six generations of the Tower family owned the Huntsmoor estate, which they called 'the old Manor', from 1696 to 1920. The picture above shows rebuilding done in 1840s but a window sill in the house had a date of 1598 on it.

The library of Huntsmoor House in 1883. Huntsmoor Park and Farm have been owned by Buckinghamshire County Council since 1937. The Manor House was demolished in 1938.

A painting which used to hang in the dining room of Huntsmoor House: *Family Group* by Phillips in 1850. It shows Christopher Tower, Lady Sophia Tower and their eldest son Christopher John Hume Tower, who was the last Tower owner of Huntsmoor. By some of their daughters' marriages they were linked to the Meekings of Richings, de Salis of Hillingdon and Iver Heath, and Dorrien-Smith of Tresco (Scilly Isles). An unmarried daughter, Lucy, worked hard for the start of the Iver Cottage Hospital and became its secretary. Lady Sophia was the daughter of Earl Brownlow and a gifted watercolour painter. Many albums of her exceptional paintings provide a unique record of Victorian life at Huntsmoor, Brafield (Bucks), Weald Hall (Essex), Ashridge (Herts), and Belton (Lincs).

The Cedar Room at Huntsmoor, with Brownlow and Adelaide Tower painted by their mother, Lady Sophia Tower in 1852. Adelaide Tower married Charles Meeking of Richings in 1863.

Next to the Swan, just off the High Street, were the houses of Swan Row, most of which were demolished in the late 1950s. This picture of 1913 shows an infant Ken Elkins on the steps of No. 1 Swan Row. At the end of the row of houses, St Stephen's Roman Catholic Church was built and opened in 1958. In the 1930s Catholics had worshipped at the Plaza Cinema in Richings Park and then used the Village Hall.

The old Fox and Pheasant in Thorney Lane in the late nineteenth or early twentieth century. It was first licensed in 1838 and was rebuilt in 1932 (see p. 90).

West Square (originally West's Square), leading to Blacksmith's Lane in the 1960s. The cottages in the distance were called Orchard Place and behind them was Burrows' farm, (or Hall's farm after a former owner). In the distance was Blacksmith's Lane which led, by a footpath between fields, to Richings Park. On the right behind the fence and hedge, was Rose Cottage, the Gospel Hall and Jones' yard.

Rose Cottage with Elizabeth Smith and her great-grandson in the 1930s. The cottage was repaired and rebuilt by her daughter, Mrs Celia Lee. It stood in West Square, behind the Garibaldi, and was formerly a coaching inn. The stables were converted into the Gospel Hall. This was all demolished in the 1970s.

Coppins, originally the house of the Copyns who lived here about 600 years ago. A Manor Roll of 1374 records 'Copynsfield'. The present residence was built by John Mitchell, a bookseller and theatrical agent who had the patronage of Queen Victoria and King Edward VII. The house was later taken by Lady Jane Churchill, a favourite lady in waiting to Queen Victoria, who personally inspected Coppins before Lady Churchill was allowed to move there! Her Majesty used to drive over by pony and chaise from Windsor to see Lady Churchill.

HRH Princess Victoria, the sister of King George V, who bought Coppins in 1925, supported many local organisations during her time in Iver. From left to right: Lady Blanche Seymour (Iver Lodge), Mr Baron Reed (Churchwarden), HRH Princess Victoria, Mrs Cobb (Vicar's wife), Miss Ward (Churchwarden). On her death in 1935, Princess Victoria left Coppins to her nephew, the Duke of Kent.

This 1930 aerial view of Thorney Lane shows in the left foreground the old Vicarage and next to it Colne House and its garden, with orchards behind, once the home of Miss Ward, who exerted a strong influence on the parish until her death in 1964. Colne House has now been demolished and new houses built on the large site which extended behind the old Vicarage to what is now Holmsdale Close. Opposite is the Church Institute (now St Peter's Centre) and churchyard.

The front entrance of Colne House, around 1950, the home for many years of Miss G.M.A. Ward, Churchwarden and daughter and grand-daughter of Vicars of Iver. Miss Ward had a signed book given to her grandmother by the famous anti-slavery campaigner, William Wilberforce. He was a great friend of the Revd Edward Ward and one day Mrs Ward, wondering how she might entertain such an eminent visitor while the Vicar was out, discovered him kneeling on the floor tying up the children's boot-laces.

The Oddfellows Arms, Iver Heath, in 1977. It was licensed in 1848 and has now been demolished. For many of its years it was run by several generations of the Cooper family.

The Old Rectory, Iver Heath, was built for £,2000 in 1865 on an acre of land given by the first Rector, George Elton. It was designed by Charles Reeks, who had also been the architect for St Margaret's Church. The house had stables (which were demolished in 1968) outbuildings and three wells.

A coach and four, about 1877, outside Heatherden Hall, the home of Dr Michael Drury-Lavin, who is sitting holding the reins, and was noted for his popular garden parties. For twenty-five years his family played an active part in the church and helped local charities. Later, during the time of Lt-Col. Grant Morden, on 3 November 1921, the treaty which created the Irish Free State was signed there, in the room which is now the main bar of the film studios. After Col. Grant Morden's death, the Heatherden Hall estate was sold by auction on 25 September 1934. It became Pinewood Film Studios in 1936.

Dromenagh, in Sevenhills Road, was once called Long Coppice and at one time owned by the Sullivan family of Richings. This house on the Dromenagh site was built for Sir Henry and Lady Lillian Yorke about 1910 and called Hillbrook Place. It was renamed Dromenagh in the 1920s. It later became a school, and was being converted into apartments when it was seriously damaged by fire.

Before 1937 the Crooked Billet public house was on a different site. This is the old Crooked Billet, on the edge of Black Park, just over the border into Langley Marish. It was a well-known alehouse for travellers to Windsor and is almost certainly much older than the date, 1753, from which the names of landlords are listed in Langley records. The Lane leading to it was once called 'Crooked Billet Lane' (now Billet Lane).

Fire-crews tackling a fire in 1946 at the new Crooked Billet at Five Points. It was later rebuilt but it no longer has a thatched roof of Norfolk reeds.

An earlier way of dealing with fire. Ancient thatch hooks, probably seventeenth-century, were found in St Peter's Church tower in 1928 by the Revd Francis Cobb. These may have been used to pull burning thatch from roofs or to pull down burning roof timbers by hauling on chains or ropes attached to the rings in the handles, which would probably have been much longer than are shown here.

Orchard Cottage (Colne House's gardener's cottage) next to Colne Lodge (Yates' Farm) in the early 1900s, with the church tower just visible in the background. For workers then accommodation went with the job and when, in the First World War, the gardener enlisted in the Navy, his wife and two infant daughters had to move out of Orchard Cottage to make way for the new gardener's family.

The houses of Leas Drive, just off the High Street, were built around 1977 on the grounds of this house, The Leas, shown here in 1928. The Lea Estate comprised land on both sides of the High Street with cottages and a farm. The house had ten bedrooms and four reception rooms and, in Victorian times, had a large staff. The Binning's, who moved to Cranmore House, were the last family to live in the Leas, which was demolished in the 1970s.

Grove House in Bangors Road was the home of Col. John Henry Patterson, seen here with his family playing croquet in their garden, c. 1906. Col. Patterson was an engineer and in 1898 he had gone to Tsavo in Kenya to help with the construction of the railway. He spent much time that year trying to protect the workers from two man-eating lions, which were preying on the men and terrifying the area. Eventually, showing much personal bravery, he shot both lions and later wrote a book, *Man-eaters of Tsavo*, which became a best-seller and is still in print. Two films have been made of his story, in 1952 and 1996.

The Red Lion Public House at Shredding Green about 1912. It was licensed before 1822. For a while, at the end of the last century, its name was changed to The Gurkha but has now reverted to the Red Lion.

Iver Grove, built between 1722 and 1724 by Sir John Vanbrugh for Lady Mohun, the wife of Charles Mohun, who was killed in a duel before the house was completed. A later owner was Admiral Lord Gambier, whose gardener, Thompson, developed the modern garden pansy there. The house was restored by the Ministry of Works in 1958-60 and resold. More recently it was the home of playwright Tom Stoppard and his wife Dr Miriam Stoppard.

The Lodge of Richings Hall. Standing outside are Bettie Roberts (the daughter of Mr Anthony of Home Farm) and her husband, D. Whitby Roberts, who was the solicitor for the Richings Park Estate. The Lodge was demolished soon after this, in the late 1980s, and houses were built on the site.

Richings Park House was owned by many who have left their mark on Iver including the Salters, Lord Bathurst, the Duke of Somerset, the Sullivans and the Meekings. The last two families were also lay rectors and so had a great influence on the life of the parish of Iver and later of Iver Heath. This house was built by the Rt Hon. John Sullivan around 1786, after an earlier house had been burnt down. During the war, the house was used by the RAF and it was demolished in 1950.

An aerial view of Richings Park from an early advertisement of the 1920s. It shows houses in Syke Ings, Wellesley Avenue, Somerset Way, Thorney Lane and Bathurst Walk being built. In the mid-distance is Thorney Lane, surrounded by fields, and the Parish Church can be seen. Richings Hall, demolished in 1950, is in the foreground. The Richings estate was sold in 1922 to the Sykes brothers by Viola Meeking (later Lady Apsley, the mother of Earl Bathurst). The land was developed for 'Country Houses near London' and advertised as being surrounded by countryside, with fresh air for the children, supplied with milk from the Richings farm and with a good train service to London. The builders felt they were offering a better way of life as well as new houses.

Newly-built houses in Thorney Lane, around 1930, looking north towards the railway bridge, before the road was widened and straightened. The large building in the background (right) is the new post office which opened in 1933.

Bathurst Walk with the Plaza Tea shop (far right), the estate agents and Wellesley Avenue, without its large trees, in the 1920s or '30s.

Eight

Special Events and Organisations

Iver's 'Welcome Home' on Saturday 8 July 1961, to the Duke and Duchess of Kent after their marriage and honeymoon. Leaving the gates of Coppins are, from the left: (front) Churchwarden Mr Binning, HRH the Duchess of Kent, the Duke of Kent, the Vicar Revd David Welander. Between the Duke and the Vicar is Mr Muir Beddall of Iver Lodge.

Iver Horticultural Society's Historical Pageant prior to their twentieth Annual Show in 1951. In the middle on her grey pony (Misty), led by a nun (Vera Povey), is 'Lady Godiva' (schoolgirl Angela Taylor). Though she was well covered with a flesh coloured swimming costume and long blonde wig, this caused quite a storm in the village at the time because many felt it was 'improper'. The route of the old Iver Lane turning left towards Bridgefoot can be seen in the mid-distance.

Iver Historical Pageant, 1951. This is the Tudor group: Maurice Povey as Henry VIII, then anticlockwise Eve Williamson as Jane Seymour, Ivy Shilston as Anne of Cleves, Eileen Shilston as Catherine of Aragon, Joan Wright as Katherine Parr, Joan Warren as Anne Boleyn, and Doreen ? as Katherine Howard.

Iver's 'From the Bookshelf' Pageant, 1952, showing characters from *Little Women* in Swan Road. From left to right: Pat Fear, Alma Sparrow, Miss Stevens, John ?, Brenda Povey, Tom Hazelgrove, Eileen Barnett, Ernest Povey, Edith Povey, Mabel Smith.

The 'Best Baby' competition at Iver and District Horticultural Society and Iver Residents' Association Show, 1949. From the left: Mrs J. Sargood and Marjory, Mrs J. Benn and Jacqueline Ann; Mrs H. Chadwell and Josephine, Mrs E. Povey and Jean, Mrs F. Archer and Andrew and Mrs V.G. Butler and Susan Ann. This was the second show since restarting the event after the war.

Iver Fair at Huntsmoor Park, 1963. The television personality Judith Chalmers, one of the judges, talks to the entrants for the Miss Iver competition. In the background, standing in front of the fence and the watching crowd, is the Revd Tony Coulson, who had just become Vicar of Iver. The Charter for Iver Fair was granted in 1351 and the 1963 fair was the first to be held for a long time.

Iver Children's Horse Show started in 1934 and later adult classes were added. It was initially held in April in Huntsmoor Park, as this 1950s picture shows, but subsequently it became a two-day show held in Langley Park in July. The proceeds initially went to Iver Cottage Hospital and still go to local charities.

The 1st Iver Guides in the 1920s or '30s. In the front are Miss Cadogan Ogg (fourth from left) and Miss Ivy Clarke (sixth from left). A story Miss Clarke told of her early days as a guide is of the never-to-be-forgotten time when she was chosen to carry the banner in church. Unfortunately both going in and coming out she managed to knock and partially demolish one of the central gas chandeliers.

March of Witness by the Choirs and Congregations of St Peter's and St Leonard's Churches on Good Friday in the late 1950s or early '60s. During the Second World War ladies were admitted to the choir for the first time as men were away on active service, although they did not robe until 1950s. Dorothy Simpson, May Smith, Lillian Weatherley, Florence James and Ivy Clarke joined and all served for many years. This picture also shows the Village sign erected to commemorate the Festival of Britain in 1951.

The 1948 Olympics were held in London. The Olympic torch was carried through Iver but had to be relit just outside the Prince of Wales public house in Iver Heath.

Olympic marathon runners passing through Iver on 24 June 1948. They ran from Windsor, where the race had been started by Queen Elizabeth, watched by King George VI, to Chiswick. The race included Britain's Olympic hopeful Jack Holden.

Chris Finnegan from Barnfield was an Olympic gold medallist in boxing in 1968. He was welcomed back home to Iver after the Mexico Olympics by other Iver residents, Miss Iver 1968/69, Sid James and Tom Hazelgrove. Tom Hazelgrove drove him to the airport on his departure for Mexico and organised his welcome-home reception at the Garibaldi.

Richings Park won the Buckinghamshire Best Kept Village competition in around 1969. It shared the title with Fulmer. A commemorative tree was planted in Bathurst Walk. In 1815 an oak tree had been planted in the old vicarage garden by the Marquis of Hertford, a pupil of the Revd Ward, to mark the victory at Waterloo but sadly this tree was cut down eighty years later.

Elizabeth R

Coronation
1953
Grand
Gala Concert

LONG MAY   SHE REIGN

Thursday, June 4th
at The Tower Arms Hall
at 8 p.m.

Programme : Price 6d.

Iver bellringers rang to mark the twenty-first birthday of the Duke of Kent on 9 October 1956 and his inheritance of the Coppins estate. From left: Jim Blandford (Vice-Captain), George Stanley (Captain), Ken Gibbons, David Rowlands (present Tower Captain), Gladys Blandford, Valerie Jolly, Bill Silvey, Althea Comber, Len Jolly. A ball was held at Coppins and a crowd of about 300 waited in the dark to see the royal guests arrive. The Queen arrived at 8.45 p.m. and asked her chauffeur to turn on the interior lights of her Rolls-Royce so that the crowd who had waited for hours could see her. She left about 3.15 a.m. and the ball continued until dawn when a bacon and egg breakfast was served.

There was a Coronation celebration concert at the Tower Arms in 1953. The programme included items by the Iverities and their Symphony Orchestra, the Townswomen's Guild, Richings Choral Society, Richings Players, Scouts and Guides, the Youth Club and the British Legion. The pianists were M.A. Robins and Daphne Smallwood.

The Old Folks' Club and its helpers at the old Village Hall in the 1940s or early '50s. Standing on the left is Mr W.J. James. On the right, the Vicar, Revd J. Cresswell, is standing in the doorway and in front of him are a group including Nora Artless, Mrs Jessop, Mrs Bristow and Mrs Dickinson. Those seated at the table include Mr Barnes, Mrs Clover, Mrs Kedge, Mrs Magston, Sally Breoles, Mabel Geary, Mrs Gillard, Mrs Diplock and Mrs Buckland.

A dinner at the Tower Arms in Thorney Lane in 1938. This was originally called the Fox and Hounds before its name was changed to link to the Tower family who owned much of Thorney and Iver between 1700 and 1900. The house was owned by the Towers until 1910 when it was sold to Victoria Brewery, Windsor.

The Richings Players

Richings Players in 1926 with *Tilly of Bloomsbury*. This was performed both at Iver and West Drayton. The cast included: Mr Leah, Mrs Seal, Rene Southcott, Edna Thorp, Leslie Dodson, Beatrice Robinson, Mrs Lawson, Frank Weston, Phyllis Jeffrey, Eric Thorp, Jessie Weston, Mr Mead, G.N. Turner, Denis Dodson. The play was produced by Eric Dodson.

Richings Players' officials. There were sixty-five founder members in 1926; of these twenty-nine were listed as 'active' and thirty-six as 'honorary'. The annual subscription was 5s and members were entitled to a reserved seat for each production unless, as active members, they were in the cast.

The Plaza Cinema was built in 1928, next to Iver station. It had the same architect and mock Tudor appearance as the rest of the estate and had its own Compton organ. Extra buses ran from Uxbridge, with a free bus service from Yiewsley, Langley and Slough. Richings Players were the first users of the cinema on 4 August with an Ian Hay play, *Happy Ending*, before the official opening on 6 August 1928. In 1939 the Plaza was sold and closed as a cinema in 1940. During the war it was used as a furniture store. It was demolished in 1962 and Wellesley Court flats were built on the site.

Richings Choral Society, 24 December 1949. From the left, back row: Jack Foster, Jim Packham, E.H. Trafford (President), Len Hoare, Harold Waite, Bert Howlett, Stanley Robinson. Front row: Mrs Mountford, Mrs Fairweather, Mrs Tracey, Kathleen Robinson, Gwen Dobbin, Peggy Bowers, Lillian Weatherley, Olive Cooke, Molly Greet (hidden), Enid Hook, Mary Greet, Audrey Hook, Joy Faint (piano) Frances Rothwell. At the front is Ralph Sutton, the Conductor and Founder of the Society.

Iver Jazz Beans Concert Party in the old Village Hall in the 1920s. The couple in the centre front are Mr and Mrs de Grey of the Elms (Langley Park Road). On the left in the back row is Jack Barber (who in 1949 completed sixty years as a bellringer). Also part of this group were Fred and Hugh Ralph and Florrie Chadwell.

The Sons of Temperance Liveners Concert Party, c. 1927. From left to right, back row: Percy Plume, George Stanley, Charlie Page, William Smith, Charles Parker. Front row: Conrad Cole, Fred Cole, Robert Barnes, Ted Cooper, Tom Barnes, Tim Grant. Conrad Cole later became a well-known church organist. George Stanley completed seventy years of bellringing in 1979. Charlie Page kept a popular nursery in Langley Park Road.

An Iver British Legion annual dinner, around 1937, held in Duttons' potting shed.

Opening of the new Village Hall complex in 1980, in West Square. HRH Princess Alexandra, a former resident of Iver, is talking to Mr Dennis Liles, the Headmaster of the Middle School, and Councillor Ros Wingrove.

Rosemary Welander presenting a bouquet to HRH the Duchess of Kent at the Church Fête at Iver Lodge on 6 June 1959. In the background are the Vicar, Revd David Welander, and Mrs Nancy Welander (seated).

Church Fête held at Iver Lodge, the home of Mr and Mrs Muir Beddall, on 6 June 1959 to raise funds for the restoration of the fabric of the Church. It was opened by HRH the Duchess of Kent and, accompanied by HRH Princess Alexandra, she spent some time visiting stalls and talking to parishioners. In the foreground from the left: Revd David Welander, -?-, Mr Binning, Princess Alexandra, Mr Muir Beddall, Mrs Welander, The Duchess of Kent (bending) and Mrs Muir Beddall.

Groups gathered in White Lodge field opposite Coppins for 11 a.m. on Saturday 8 July 1961 to welcome home to Iver the Duke and Duchess of Kent on their return from honeymoon. After an address, gifts were presented and then there was an opportunity for them to meet representative members of Iver's organisations, who were gathered in a semicircle round the dais.

Ladies of Iver Heath's Trefoil Guild ready to welcome home the Duke and Duchess. From the left, back row: Jean Ayres, -?-, 'Freddy' Stapley, 'Tommy' Parker, Brenda Hodgins, Brenda Collins, Molly Brecknall. Front row: Jean Chaston, Helen Hargreaves, Margaret Worcester, Eve Samson, Miss Ogg, Edna Vivash, Beryl Horsman.

Iver Unity FC, Nicholay Cup, 1932/33. From the left, back row: -?-, ? Woodley, Ernie Povey, -?-, -?-, -?-, ? Godleman. Front row: ? Johnson, -?-, -?-, -?-, -?-, Johnny Brench, Bill Spring. Football was played in the Nicholay's field (of Iver Grove) in Langley Park Road. As well as Iver Unity, there was also an Iver Celtic team. Mrs Nicholay had been a long-standing supporter and patron of Iver football and cricket.

The Cadets of Temperance, Iver Section, at the District Sports. They were the winners of a shield in the early 1930s. From left to right, back row: Irene Wharton, -?-, -?-, -?-, Wilfred Munday, Teddy Robbins, George Watling, Henry Munday, -?-, Gwen Thetford. Middle row: Sylvia Harris, -?-, Joan Wharton, -?-, Rosie Jessop, Peggy Hambidge, Josie Gathergood, -?-, -?-, Georgie Gathergood. Front : -?-, -?-, -?-, Barbara Pearce, Barbara Gathergood, Reg Munday (with shield), Gwyn Stanley, Phyllis Buckland, -?-, I. Simpson, Gladys Lyford.

Iver Football Club, who won the local Premier League trophy in the late 1920s. One of the managers, Henry Charles Povey (front, far right), had twin sons playing – James (back row, third from left) and Arthur (middle row, fourth from left).

Sport for all at Richings Park. When the estate was built in 1925, Richings Park Estates Ltd left the central area of about 9 acres for sports facilities, and tennis, cricket, hockey and bowls clubs began. Richings Park Sports Club was eventually formed and was fortunate enough to be able to acquire the freehold of the ground in 1946. A pavilion, lounge, bars, car park and other amenities have been added over the years.

Acknowledgements

Sincere thanks are due to all those, past and present, who have helped by providing photographs or information for this book: Fred and Gwyn Archer, Andrew Bailey, Alastair Beddall, K.S. Block, Anthony Boswell, Peggy Bowers, Paul Bromley, Mrs Brum, Tessa and Richard Buckley, Josie Burford, Brian Butler, Flicky Caisley, Francis Cobb, Violette Cochrane, Edna Cockram, Jack Cresswell, Mick Crowther, Tillie Dancey, Colin Davenport, Alma Davies, Norman Edwards, Ken and Jo Elkins, Peter Elliott, Bill Fewings, Mrs Files, S.H. Freese, Doris Goode, Fred Goodman; Paul Graham and Simon Hill of the Iver and District Countryside Association; Gillian Granlund, Anna Hansen, Helen and John Hargreaves, Joan Hazelgrove, Michael and Maureen James, Joe and Anne King, Bob and Peggy Lambert, Adam Lovejoy, Michael Maher, Mrs McGoona, Jane Milward, Henry Munday, Mrs Muir Beddall, Ken Pearce, Michael Peel, Gavin and Joy Pomeroy, Arthur and Barbara Potter, Maurice Povey, Iris Preston, Althea Read, David Reynish, Bettie Roberts, Ted and Doreen Roberts, Kathleen Robinson, David, Peggy, Sandra and Stanley Rowlands, Douglas and Eileen Rust, Pat Sawdon, Adrian and Anthea Secker, P.R. Shah, George Sibley, Brian and Gill Skinner, F.J. Standerwick, George Stanley, Jenny Steele, Mrs Talbot, John and Pauline Telfer, Alastair Tower, Bill Tower, Pam Tower, Joy Troke, Mary Turvill, W.H. Ward, Brian Weatherley, David Welander, Margaret Wilkins, Jackie Wilson, Janet Winter, Wendy Wright.

The considerable help given by Roger Bettridge, County Archivist, and James Venn, photographer, is very much appreciated. The permission of the Centre for Buckinghamshire Studies to reproduce PHX5 photographs as follows is most gratefully acknowledged: 44/2 (p. 40b), 226/4, 2, 3 (pp. 89a, 89b, 90a), 186/1 (p. 90b), 212 (pp. 91a, b, 92a, b) 77/2 (p. 128) 77/4 (p. 26) 77/5 (p. 4).

The kind permission to include photographs from the *Buckinghamshire Advertiser*, Lloyds of London, *Slough & Windsor Observer* Group and the *Uxbridge Gazette* is also greatly appreciated.

Considerable effort has been made to try to identify photographers and establish copyright. Permission to reproduce photographs has been obtained where required. However, if unknowingly I have omitted to contact anyone whose photograph has been included, please accept my most sincere apologies.

Stella Rowlands

Slough Road, Iver Heath, looking towards Uxbridge, on 11 May 1928.

IVER, BUCKINGHAMSHIRE

Once surrounded by fields and orchards, the villages of
Iver, Iver Heath and Richings Park have seen many
changes over the last century. From their origins as quiet
farming communities, this volume recalls the importance
of two other industries – brick-making and film-making –
and records the influence they have had in shaping the
history of the area.

Renowned for being the home of Pinewood Film Studios
and for a Royal residence at Coppins, Iver has seen many
famous faces, but it is the everyday people and places that
really provide an insight into what life was once like.
Illustrated with 230 archive pictures, this intriguing
collection visits the cottage hospital built by public
subscription, country houses, churches and schools, roads,
transport, fêtes and pageants. Local characters are also
remembered, including the vicar who flew over his parish
in the early days of flight, the Girl Guide who demolished
a gas chandelier, the engineer who shot man-eating lions
and the children who worked in the brickfields.

Accompanied by informative text, *Around Iver* is a
valuable pictorial history which will reawaken nostalgic
memories for some, while offering a unique glimpse of the
past for others.

The sale of this book helps the work of the Thames Valley Hospice.

IMAGES *of England*
IS PART OF THE *Archive Photographs* SERIES

TEMPUS PUBLISHING LIMITED
THE MILL, BRIMSCOMBE PORT,
STROUD, GLOUCESTERSHIRE, GL5 2QG

£11.99

ISBN 0-7524-2862-4

9 780752 428628

HAUNTED
ESSEX

CARMEL KING